READING WITH OLD STYLE CONJURE CARDS

STARR CASAS

READING
WITH
OLD STYLE
CONJURE
CARDS

STARR CASAS

PENDRAIG Publishing
Los Angeles, CA 91040

Reading with Old Style Conjure Cards
by Starr Casas
First Edition © 2013
by PENDRAIG Publishing
All rights reserved.

No part of this publication may be reproduced, stored in a retrieval system or transmitted in any form or by any means, electronic, mechanical, photocopying, recording or otherwise without the prior written permission of the copyright holder, except brief quotation in a review.

Cover Design,
Interior Images,   Jo-Ann Byers Mierzwicki
Typeset & Layout

PENDRAIG Publishing
Los Angeles, CA 91040
www.PendraigPublishing.com
Printed in the United States of America

ISBN: 978-1-936922-60-4

Warning!

Any reader who uses the work
within this book
does so entirely at their own risk.

The author and publisher accept no liability
if the work does not have the desired effect

or

if adverse effects are caused.

TABLE OF CONTENTS

Introduction	11
History of Reading the Playing Cards	15
Getting the Cards Ready	21
How to Work the Cards	27
The Card Lay Outs	33
The Cards	39
Ace of Diamonds	40
King of Diamonds	41
Queen of Diamonds	42
Jack of Diamonds	43
Ten of Diamonds	44
Nine of Diamonds	45
Eight of Diamonds	46
Seven of Diamonds	47
Six of Diamonds	48

Five of Diamonds	49
Four of Diamonds	50
Three of Diamonds	51
Two of Diamonds	52
Ace of Hearts	53
King of Hearts	54
Queen of Hearts	55
Jack of Hearts	56
Ten of Hearts	57
Nine of Hearts	58
Eight of Hearts	59
Seven of Hearts	60
Six of Hearts	61
Five of Hearts	62
Four of Hearts	63
Three of Hearts	64
Two of Hearts	65
Ace of Clubs	66
King of Clubs	67
Queen of Clubs	68
Jack of Clubs	69
Ten of Clubs	70
Nine of Clubs	71
Eight of Clubs	72
Seven of Clubs	73
Six of Clubs	74
Five of Clubs	75
Four of Clubs	76
Three of Clubs	77
Two of Clubs	78
Ace of Spades	79
King of Spades	80
Queen of Spades	81

Jack of Spades	82
Ten of Spades	83
Nine of Spades	84
Eight of Spades	85
Seven of Spades	86
Six of Spades	87
Five of Spades	88
Four of Spades	89
Three of Spades	90
Two of Spades	91
Joker	92
Card Combinations	93
Timing in Readings	99
Closing	101
Other Resources	103
About the Author	107

Introduction

When my mama passed in 1987 we found an old deck of playing cards in one of her chest of drawers. I can't claim that those were my mama's cards; I think they were and she was real tricky at keeping things hidden. I never saw her with cards; I can say that she would look into water, a coffee cup or the flame of a lamp because I caught her doing it. I saw her with my own eyes. She did tie an old button on a string for me to play with when I was young {I now know that it was a pendulum} that she made for me. I've always had a thing about strings, almost every baby picture I have of myself I'm holding cotton twine. I work well with the pendulum. When I was around thirteen a lady I babysat for gave me an Ouija board for my birthday. I was so excited about that board; but the first time I used the board it scared the hell out of me. My mama burned it and we buried it in the backyard. I remember Mama saying the spirit in that board did not rest well. I have never touched another board.

One summer I went with my cousin to her Aunt's house to spend the summer. One day we were all sitting around the kitchen table when her aunt asked if we wanted her to tell our future. Of course we did we were young girls and wanted to know who we would marry. Once she read them for us we wanted to learn to read them. She wrote down all the different meanings and we practiced all summer. Every day we would lay the cards out. After a while we both just knew what the cards were saying to us. She taught us how to open up to spirit so we could understand the message the cards were giving. When we went back home after summer break I continued to practice reading the cards; my cousin stopped reading them and I would read hers for her. I haven't spoken to her in over forty years due to the last card reading I gave her.

She met this guy and fell head over heels in love. She came to me for a reading. I was honest and told her it wouldn't last; he would cheat and abuse her. She got the red ass and so did I so we didn't speak for about ten years. Then I ran into her at the store one day. When we were young we were very close. I really missed her; I was glad to see her. We went out for dinner and a drink. Damn if we didn't get into an argument about her husband. She blamed me because I let her marry him. Her words "I should have done something to stop her" I have not spoken to her since nor will I ever. For a long time I wouldn't read for anyone except myself. Then I started reading for family and friends; then onto reading professionally. The one thing that has always stuck with me is you have to be careful when you are reading for your friends especially if it has to do with love issues.

I'm a no B.S. reader and conjure worker; I don't beat around the bush. This is hard for some folks to take, but I'm not gonna feed them a bunch of bull. It is what it is. You can't make a silk purse out of a sow's ear; so if the guy is no good then that's what I say. If a client comes to me for help and I see the job won't work I tell them that too. The whole time I was putting this deck of cards together I was praying and calling on spirit to help whoever reads these cards understand the whole picture. Reading playing cards has become a lost art. I have tried to learn to read Tarot cards with no success. I have one deck out of about thirty decks that I can understand a little. I think everyone should be able to read the playing cards if they want too.

This deck of cards is not just any ole deck of cards. You can actually do work with this deck of cards to bring change into your life and your loved ones lives. I worked with my ancestors and the spirits that walk with me; I prayed that spirit would lead the reader into the right direction that they should go when they consult this deck of cards. I think I achieved that goal. I hope you enjoy the OSC card kit and that the spirits of the cards speak to you.

Momma Starr

History of Reading the Playing Cards

Old timey conjure workers and spiritual readers have always worked with the playing cards. No one knows for sure how or when it started but regular playing cards {also called poker cards} have always been around. They evolved from the Tarot card decks into what they are now and have a special meaning to conjure workers and gifted readers alike. Ever since the first conjure man/woman flipped the cards over they took on a special meaning for two headed doctors and conjure workers. In traditional conjure work there are special meanings and works for the playing cards that you won't find elsewhere. In fact the playing cards are a work in themselves. In conjure when you work with the playing cards you can reverse the outcome revealed in that card. There are special setups and prayers you can work with to better your circumstances and remove any blocks that come in your life. If you see blocks when dealing the deals there are Road Opener works you can do and vice versa.

The way I was taught is that the playing cards tell a story. You as the reader only need to let your ancestors and the Spirit's that walk with you open your eyes so you can discern the story and how it applies to your life. Some people say there are drawbacks to reading the playing cards because there are no pictures and you have to memorize the numbers. I disagree because anytime you are doing a reading you are opening yourself up to your ancestors and your Spirit's. I feel the ancestors and the spirits that walk with you give you the information to help you or your client find the right direction to go. If you are open to Spirit and have a strong relationship with your Ancestors then you will know what your ancestors and your Spirits are saying whether reading the playing cards, throwing the bones, or looking into a cup of water. You have to trust in God or your Higher Power, your ancestors and let the Spirit's guide you if you want to be a good reader.

Divination has always been around and goes

back to biblical times. You'll even find bone throwing in the Bible. As you can see in the passage God authorized Joshua to cast lots {in Conjure we call it throwing the bones} so the lands around Judea could be divided fairly. If you also read Ezekiel 21 verses 18-23 God tells Ezekiel that the king of Babylon will cast arrows at the crossroads in front of Jerusalem. In this chapter God specifically mentions how the arrows tell the King to capture Jerusalem and enslave the Hebrews. Something that is easy to overlook in this chapter is that God allows this to occur and influences the arrows to do his will.

Ezekiel 21 V18-23

18 The word of the Lord came to me again, saying:

19 "And son of man, appoint for yourself two ways for the sword of the king of Babylon to go; both of them shall go from the same land. Make a sign; put it at the head of the road to the city.

20 Appoint a road for the sword to go to Rabbah of the Ammonites, and to Judah, into fortified Jerusalem.

21 For the king of Babylon stands at the parting of the road, at the fork of the two roads, to use divination: he shakes the arrows, he consults the images, he looks at the liver.

22 In his right hand is the divination for Jerusalem: to set up battering rams, to call for a slaughter, to lift the voice with shouting, to set battering rams against the gates, to heap up a siege mound, and to build a wall.

23 For the king of Babylon stands at the parting of the way, at the head of the two ways, to use divination. He shakes the arrows; he consults the teraphim; he looks at the liver.

Divination has always been around and goes back to biblical times. You'll even find bone throwing in the Bible. For example in Joshua 18 verses 5, 6, & 8 Joshua casts lots to divide his ancestral lands between the seven tribes of Israel.

Joshua 18 V5-6

"You are to divide the land into seven parts. Judah is to remain in its territory on the south and the tribes of Joseph in their territory on the north. After you have written descriptions of the seven parts of the land, bring them here to me and I will cast lots for you in the presence of the LORD our God."

Joshua 18 V 8

As the men started on their way to map out the land, Joshua instructed them,

"Go and make a survey of the land and write a description of it. Then return to me, and I will cast lots for you here at Shiloh in the presence of the LORD."

As you can see in the passage God authorized Joshua to cast lots {in Conjure we call it throwing the bones} so the lands around Judea could be divided fairly. The first thing to remember is that when you are doing divination you are opening yourself up. You need to protect yourself so you don't draw something unwanted into your life. Before I do any consultation I say a prayer to God, my ancestors and all my spirits that walk with me for protection and strength. I then ask my Ancestors to guide me and show me the truth. I petition my dead to protect me while I consult the client and keep me open where I always see the truth. Divination is a part of God's work and there's nothing evil about it even though some Christians and religious folks may think otherwise. As long as you are calling on God or your personal Higher Power and petitioning your ancestors you are fine.

Proverbs 16 V 33

"The lot is cast into the lap, but its every decision is from the LORD."

In Genesis 44 V4-5 we see that Joseph had a reading cup.

4 When they had gone out of the city, and were not yet far off, Joseph said to his steward, "Get up, follow the men; and when you overtake them, and say to them, 'Why have you repaid evil for good?

5 Is not this the one from which my lord drinks, and with which he indeed practices divination? You have done evil in so doing.

V 14-15

14 So Judah and his brothers came to Joseph's house, and he was still there; and they fell before him on the ground.

15 And Joseph said to them, "What deed is this you have done? Did you not know that such a man as I can certainly practice divination?"

16 Then Judah said, "What shall we say to my lord? What shall we speak? Or how shall we clear ourselves? God has found out the iniquity of your servants; here we are my lord's slaves, both we and he also with whom the cup was found."

Getting the Cards Ready

Just like any other tool you work with before you put the tool to work you have to dress the tool and bless it. These cards are no different. I have heard a lot of different things from readers over the years about folks touching their cards. Some say the cards will stop reading for them or it pulls the power from the deck or its bad luck, the tales go on and on. Well you don't have to worry about that with this deck because your ancestors and the spirits that walk with you will be in the deck. They always have your back. So Suzie Q or big bubba next door can handle the deck and it won't make a difference, that's why these are called *"Conjure Cards"*. The ancestors and the spirit that walk with you cover your deck.

You may be saying *"hhmm Momma Starr, I don't know anything about working with my ancestors"* well of course I'm gonna help you out. Everyone should know how to honor their dead. Our ancestors paved the way for us to be where we are today. I think that my Great Grandma, my Grandma and my mama all prayed for better times when they were picking cotton under the scorching sun in the cotton field and working under the tobacco barn. Until the day my mama died her hands still held scares from picking cotton. So why in the world wouldn't they help us after they passed on? The love is still there, the wanting us to better ourselves is still there. I know some folks say you shouldn't petition your ancestors for help; you should just honor them. My question has always been why not?

Our ancestors have worked hard their whole lives they have an invested interest in our lives.

Why in the world would you keep them on an altar at arm's length? With that being said the first thing you need to do is to set up a small or large space for your ancestors, this can be your blood kin or folks who are family because you love them. Make sure you clean the area good before you set up your altar or table which ever you prefer. You can make a spray by adding a cap of ammonia to a spray bottle of water. All you have to do is pray your petition over the bottle; then spray and wipe. You can cover your altar with whatever you have on hand. I have mine covered with a piece of the shroud that came off my sisters casket. As you can see it is purple.

If you have them you can add photos, things that meant something to them, you decide what goes on there. The only things that are a must are a cool glass of water, a bible, smoke and light. Once you have your altar set up, give them a cool drink and a light. Tap three times either with a conjure stick, your foot or by rapping the altar and call them to you. This is how I do it.

I call on God the Father,
God the Son, God the Holy Spirit.

I call on ALL my ancestors
known and unknown
who are WILLING to come to me.

I offer you this altar in your honor,

*that you may rest here
and be remembered.*
Come NOW to your honored place.

Then you go on and offer them the water, light, smoke and just talk to them from your heart. You can say prayers for them or even play music for them; what matters is that you care enough about them to give them their own space within your home. No hocus pocus needed just plain ole caring about your blood kin will do the trick to pull them to you. They already walk with you; you just have to invite them into your life. Some folks have a fear of the dead my mama always told us *"it's not the dead you have to worry about it's the living"*. None of us have ever feared the dead or the graveyard because we were raised to honor and respect both. Once you have an ongoing flow with them where you hear them when they speak it's time to give them your cards so they can become a part of the deck.

Hold your cards up close to your mouth and say your birth name into the cards three times. Then you lay out a white handkerchief on your altar; place your cards in the center of the hankie. You tap three times on top of your deck, on each tap you call on your ancestors and you petition them to fill the deck with their knowledge and power so that you will always understand what the cards are telling you. Then you set a tea light that you have prayed over on top of the cards, repeat your petition to your ancestors and light the tea light. Repeat this process for seven days, on the seventh day after the tea light burns out take up your handkerchief and your deck. Now is the time to test them. Lay the hankie out, call on the trinity and your ancestors, petition them to come to you, then hold the deck up to your mouth and say your birth name into the cards. Then shuffle the cards and lay them out. I like to keep a bowl of blue water and light going on my table where I read, I have found that is helps the ancestors sit at the table. After you finished your first reading cover the cards with the hankie and put your cards back on your altar. At bed time that night take them and put them in your pillow case. You do this for seven nights also, laying the cards out daily and placing them on your ancestor altar during the day.

You should now have a very strong link with your deck. Every time you do a reading before you lay the first card down you call on the Trinity and your ancestors, then you say your name into the cards three times and petition for a true reading. At first you need to ask questions you already know the answers too, this way you can be sure the cards are reading true. If for some reason they don't then repeat the process until you have a strong bond between yourself, your ancestors and your deck.

How to Work the Cards

There are many ways that you can do spiritual work with this deck of cards. When I was taught to read the cards as a young girl I was taught to place a picture of Jesus or the Holy family under the card that represented me or the person being read for. This not only helps to get a true reading but it keeps the spirit of the reading positive. Below you will see a couple of different layouts that you can use when you are either working for yourself or a client. These layouts can be used for cleansing, protection, attraction, crossing, and prosperity work. It all depends on the candles and the card you choose for the set up; also the bible verse and the petition prayed over the work.

This layout is what I call a *straight shot* because everything is in a straight line, some ole workers call this *burning hard* and some of them think that if you burn to often in this layout it can make things happen that aren't always good.

The center card represents the target and is laid down first.

Then if you are trying to bring something or do a healing or remove a crossed condition you would lay the second card to the right then the last card goes to the left.

But if this is a *hard work* then you would lay the second card to the left first and the last card to the right to nail em down.

This layout is a one card layout that can be worked for:

Prosperity, reversal, uncrossing or healing.

Again it depends on how you place the candles around the card.

Place the targets photo or name under the card for the best results.

The above picture depicts a cross layout working with the cards. This layout can be for positive change or not so positive change. It all depends on the cards being worked with and the way you lay the cards down.

The card in the center represents the target. Or the person the work is being done for or on.

To open the way you would lay cards 1,2,3, down first then the right hand card is laid down the left hand card.

Now if you are blocking something or someone the left hand card is laid down then the right hand card. This is called closing the roads.

So right to left is opening a targets roads and left to right is closing them as in locking them down.

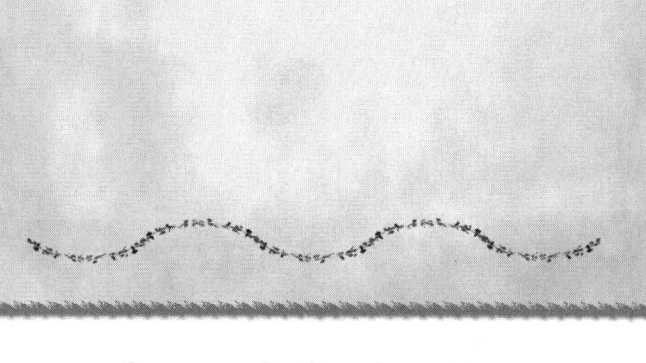

The Card Lay Outs

Below are the layouts I work with the most, the three {3} card layout is for quick reading. Always remember that it matters how you lay the cards down when you are dealing with a job. Right to left opens, left to right closes.

The three {3}card layout is for a quick reading or a *quickie* as I call it.

Use this lay out for one question readings.

The cards are laid out with the target or the person getting the consult in the center.

Then the next card is laid on the right side and the last is laid on the left.

This layout is great when you are trying to find out if you have a crossed condition or if you have been conjuered.

I use the *crossroads layout* below for most of my readings.

The first card laid down represents the person the reading is for.

Then you lay a card at the top,

Then over the person,

Then bottom,

Then right to left.

The next two lay outs are the *triangle layouts*.

Start from right to left when laying the cards out. I don't think the layout really matters; I think what matters is your connection to your ancestors and your spirits also it depends on how in tuned you are with your ancestors. These layouts are not written in stone they are the ones I use for my readings.

In the layouts above you see that they are basically the same lay out only slightly different. In this layout you build the layout around the target. If you could pick up the photo of Jesus you would find a petition written underneath it. That petition is the foundation of the reading. Jesus is a great healer; for example a reading for a client showed signs of illness; the second layout with the petition under Jesus would be to find out what could be done to help prevent the health issue.

In both layouts the card that represents the target is laid down first. If you are doing a consult then you would lay the target {the person having the reading done} down as the first card. You can also lay the card on top of their photo if they are not there for the consult.

The next card laid down is the right hand card, then the left. This represents what is going on right now in the person's life.

The next layout of the cards is the top, this represents the past; what caused the situation. These are laid out from right to left.

The last set of cards is what I call the answer layout. These tell you what can be done to help the situation. You can either just pull one card which is placed under the target or you can pull three for a more in-depth answer.

This is how you lay the cards for a consult; now if you are doing a work on or for the target then the laying of the cards depend on what you want the outcome to be. Either way the target is the first card you lay down.

If you are going to do a positive work for a client working with this lay out then you would pick all positive cards and lay them out in the order given above.

These would be hearts for love, diamonds and some clubs for prosperity; just to give you an idea.

Now if you are doing a work that is a bit darker then you would lay all the cards down from left to right. This will shut down all their roads and block them.

In either set up you would burn a set of four candles around the layout.

The candles you burn and the way you set the candles depends on the reason for doing the work.

These are conjure cards, they are meant to be worked with as well as being read.

The Cards

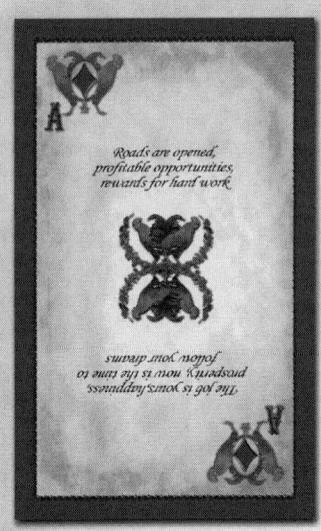

Ace of Diamonds

Roads are opened, profitable opportunities, rewards for hard work

The job is yours, happiness, prosperity, now is the time to follow your dreams

Jeremiah 1 V 9-10

Then the LORD reached out his hand and touched my mouth and said to me, "I have put my words in your mouth. See, today I appoint you over nations and kingdoms to uproot and tear down, to destroy and overthrow, to build and to plant."

King of Diamonds

A fair haired man, stubborn vindictive, powerful, and he is dangerous when he is crossed, Career achievements.

Your roads are opened proceed faster you are moving in the right direction do not detour from your path

Job 36 V 7-11

"He does not take his eyes off the righteous; he enthrones them with kings and exalts them forever. But if people are bound in chains, held fast by cords of affliction, he tells them what they have done that they have sinned arrogantly. He makes them listen to correction and commands them to repent of their evil. If they obey and serve him, they will spend the rest of their days in prosperity and their years in contentment."

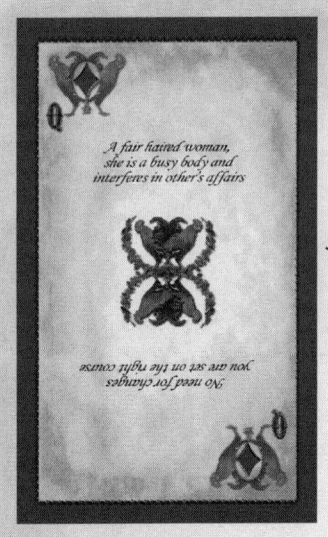

Queen of Diamonds

A fair haired woman, she is a busy body and interferes in other's affairs

No need for changes you are set on the right course

---

2 Corinthians 9 V 6-8

"Remember this: Whoever sows sparingly will also reap sparingly, and whoever sows generously will also reap generously. Each of you should give what you have decided in your heart to give, not reluctantly or under compulsion, for God loves a cheerful giver. And God is able to bless you abundantly, so that in all things at all times, having all that you need, you will abound in every good work."

Jack of Diamonds

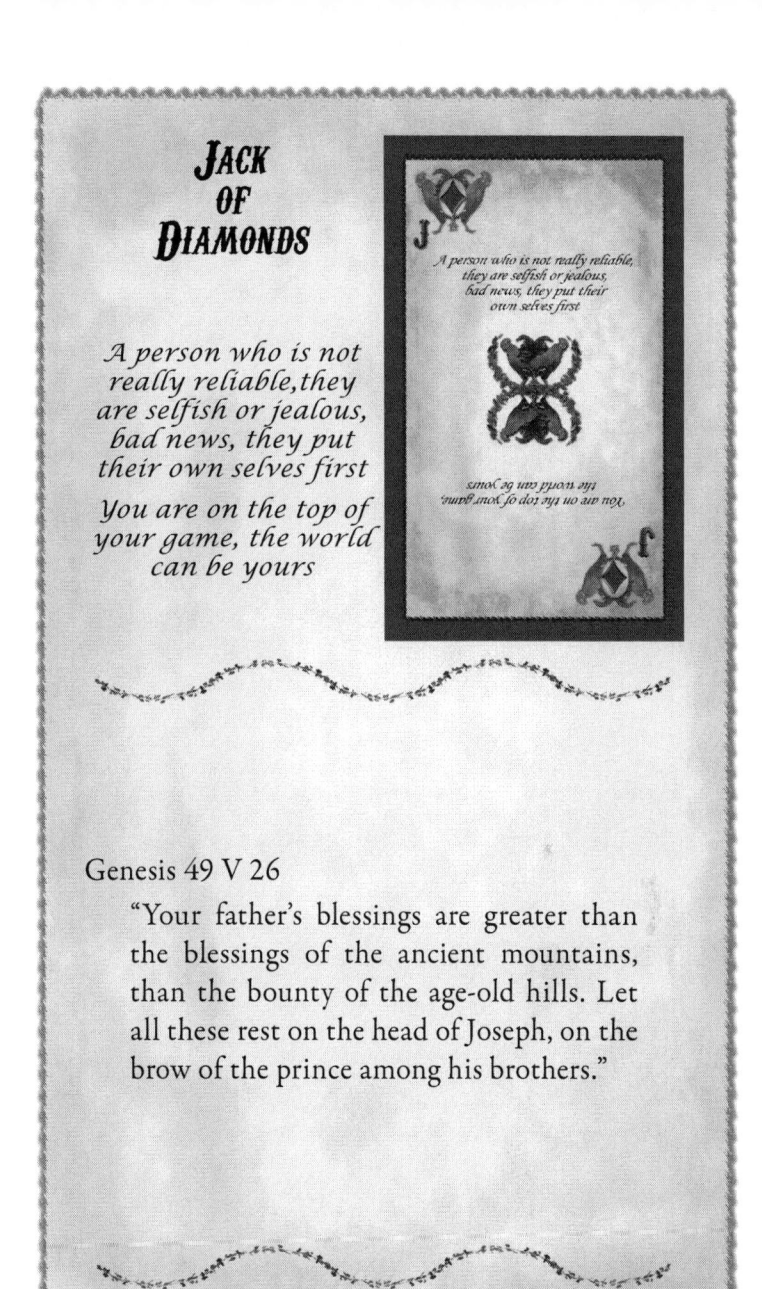

A person who is not really reliable, they are selfish or jealous, bad news, they put their own selves first

You are on the top of your game, the world can be yours

Genesis 49 V 26

"Your father's blessings are greater than the blessings of the ancient mountains, than the bounty of the age-old hills. Let all these rest on the head of Joseph, on the brow of the prince among his brothers."

Ten of Diamonds

Success in reference to your question

Total success, money, love, joy

Genesis 30 V 43

"In this way the man grew exceedingly prosperous and came to own large flocks, and female and male servants, and camels and donkeys."

Nine of Diamonds

Opportunities arise, don't go into partnerships you will do better acting on your own

It's your time for success

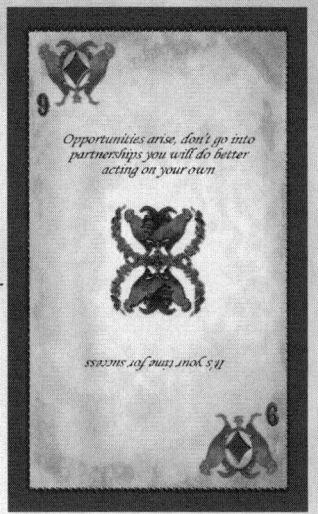

Romans 16 V 17-19

"I urge you, brothers and sisters, to watch out for those who cause divisions and put obstacles in your way that are contrary to the teaching you have learned. Keep away from them. For such people are not serving our Lord Christ, but their own appetites. By smooth talk and flattery they deceive the minds of naive people. Everyone has heard about your obedience, so I rejoice because of you; but I want you to be wise about what is good, and innocent about what is evil."

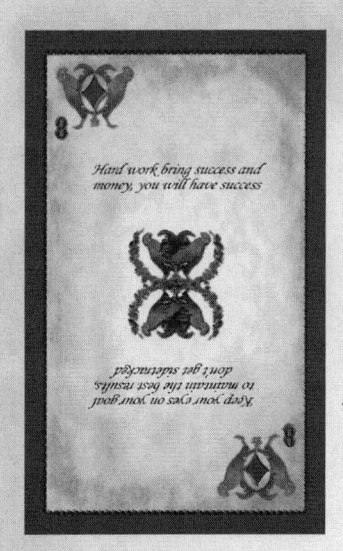

Eight of Diamonds

Hard work bring success and money, you will have success

Keep your eyes on your goal to maintain the best results, don't get sidetracked

Deuteronomy 8 V 17-18

> You may say to yourself, "My power and the strength of my hands have produced this wealth for me." But remember the LORD your God, for it is he who gives you the ability to produce wealth, and so confirms his covenant, which he swore to your ancestors, as it is today.

Seven of Diamonds

Lies, gossip, unlucky gambler, criticism, you spend more money than you have

If you draw this card you need to take a set of {5} cleaning bathes and do some road openers

Proverbs 13 V 11

> Wealth gained hastily will dwindle, but whoever gathers little by little will increase it.

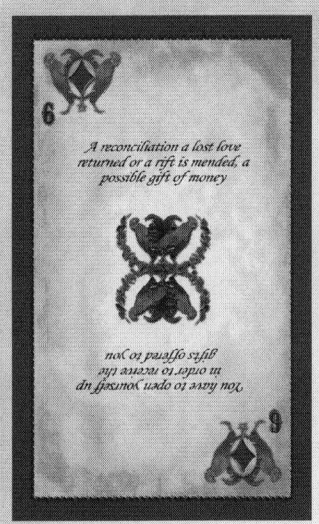

Six of Diamonds

A reconciliation a lost love returned or a rift is mended, a possible gift of money

You have to open yourself up in order to receive the gifts offered to you

Isaiah 60 V 17-18

> I will make peace your governor and well-being your ruler.
>
> No longer will violence be heard in your land, nor ruin or destruction within your borders, but you will call your walls Salvation and your gates Praise."

2 Chronicles 31 V 10

> and Azariah the chief priest, from the family of Zadok, answered, "Since the people began to bring their contributions to the temple of the LORD, we have had enough to eat and plenty to spare, because the LORD has blessed his people, and this great amount is left over."

Five of Diamonds

In a general way it means unexpected news, or success in business enterprises.

You are miserable, you need to be grateful for your blessings, stop worrying about what you don't have

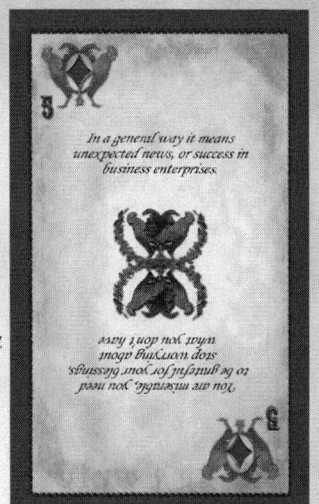

Joshua 1 V 7-9

> "Be strong and very courageous. Be careful to obey all the law my servant Moses gave you; do not turn from it to the right or to the left, that you may be successful wherever you go. Keep this Book of the Law always on your lips; meditate on it day and night, so that you may be careful to do everything written in it. Then you will be prosperous and successful. Have I not commanded you? Be strong and courageous. Do not be afraid; do not be discouraged, for the LORD your God will be with you wherever you go."

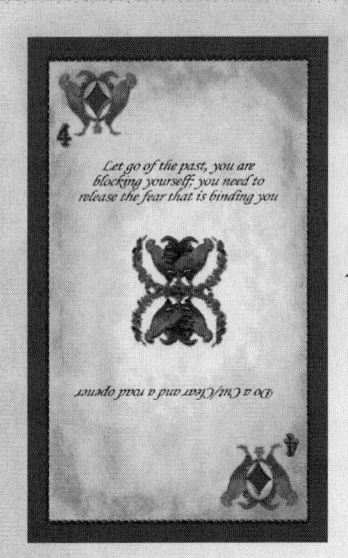

Four of Diamonds

Let go of the past, you are blocking yourself; you need to release the fear that is binding you

Do a Cut/Clear and a road opener

Deuteronomy 31:6

> Be strong and courageous. Do not fear or be in dread of them, for it is the Lord your God who goes with you. He will not leave you or forsake you.

Three of Diamonds

You need to keep a cool head quarrels, domestic disagreements

Do a peaceful home vigil

Ecclesiastes 4 V 9-12

Two are better than one, because they have a good return for their labor: If either of them falls down, one can help the other up. But pity anyone who falls and has no one to help them up. Also, if two lie down together, they will keep warm.

But how can one keep warm alone? Though one may be overpowered, two can defend themselves. A cord of three strands is not quickly broken.

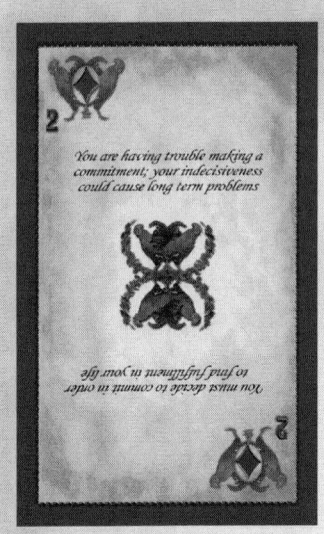

Two of Diamonds

You are having trouble making a commitment; your indecisiveness could cause long term problems

You must decide to commit in order to find fulfillment in your life

Isaiah 55 V 11-12

"So is my word that goes out from my mouth: It will not return to me empty, but will accomplish what I desire and achieve the purpose for which I sent it. You will go out in joy and be led forth in peace."

Ace of Hearts

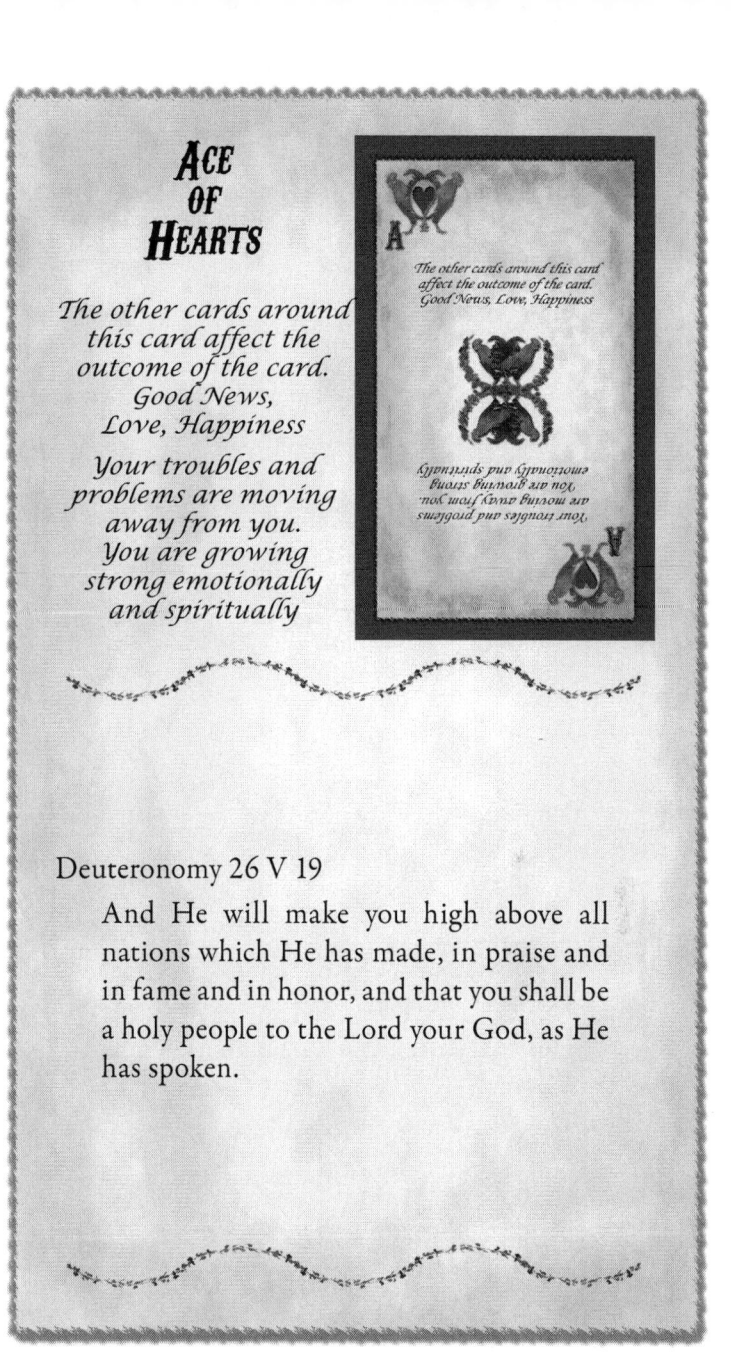

The other cards around this card affect the outcome of the card.
Good News,
Love, Happiness

Your troubles and problems are moving away from you. You are growing strong emotionally and spiritually

Deuteronomy 26 V 19

And He will make you high above all nations which He has made, in praise and in fame and in honor, and that you shall be a holy people to the Lord your God, as He has spoken.

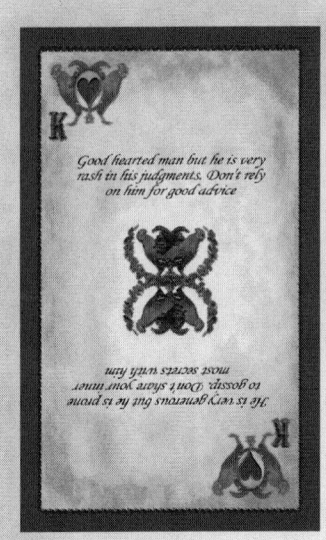

King of Hearts

Good hearted man but he is very rash in his judgments. Don't rely on him for good advice

He is very generous but he is prone to gossip. Don't share your inner most secrets with him

Song of Songs 1 V 12-14

While the king was at his table, my perfume spread its fragrance. My beloved is to me a sachet of myrrh resting between my breasts. My beloved is to me a cluster of henna blossoms from the vineyards of En Gedi.

Queen of Hearts

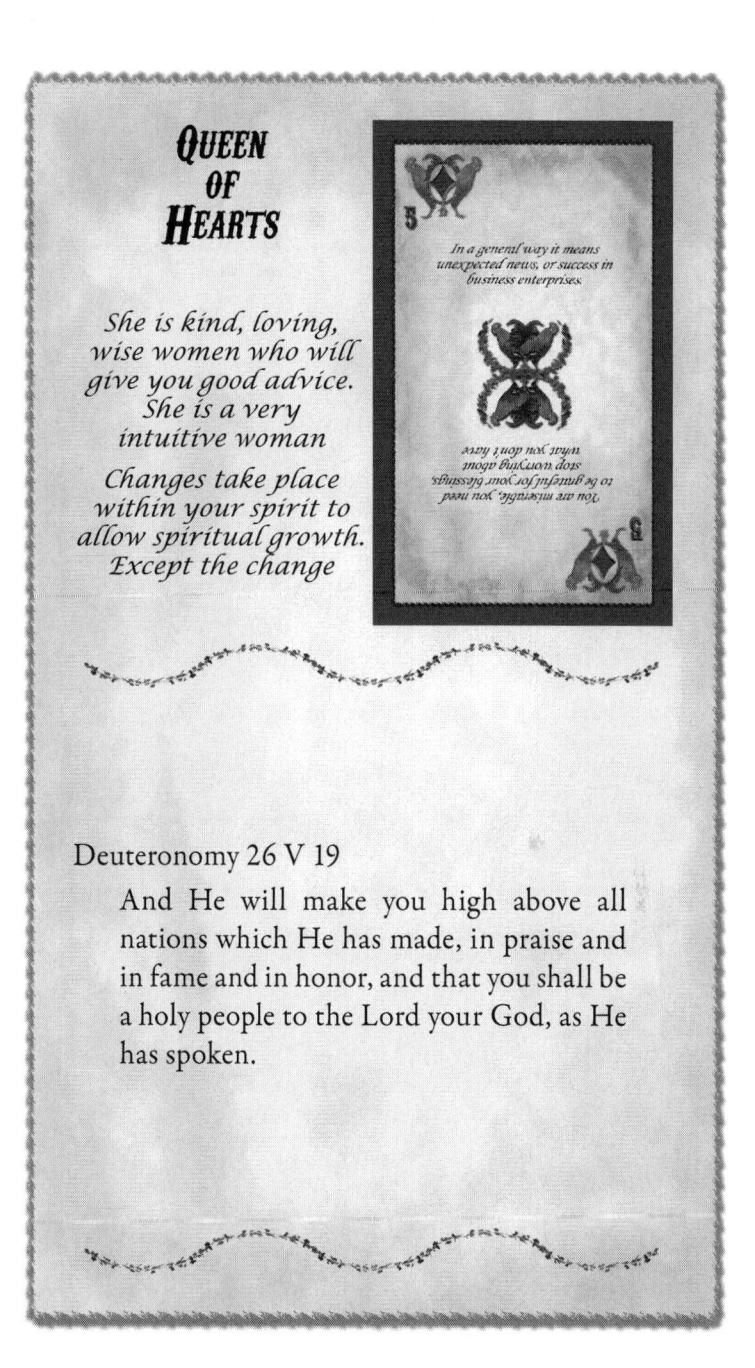

She is kind, loving, wise women who will give you good advice. She is a very intuitive woman

Changes take place within your spirit to allow spiritual growth. Except the change

In a general way it means unexpected news, or success in business enterprises.

You are miserable, you need to be grateful for your blessings, stop worrying about what you don't have.

Deuteronomy 26 V 19

And He will make you high above all nations which He has made, in praise and in fame and in honor, and that you shall be a holy people to the Lord your God, as He has spoken.

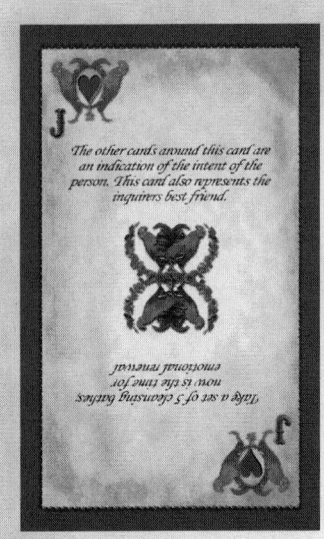

Jack of Hearts

The other cards around this card are an indication of the intent of the person. This card also represents the inquirers best friend.

Take a set of 5 cleansing bathes; now is the time for emotional renewal

---

Romans 12 V 2

Do not be conformed to this world, but be transformed by the renewal of your mind, that by testing you may discern what is the will of God, what is good and acceptable and perfect.

Ten of Hearts

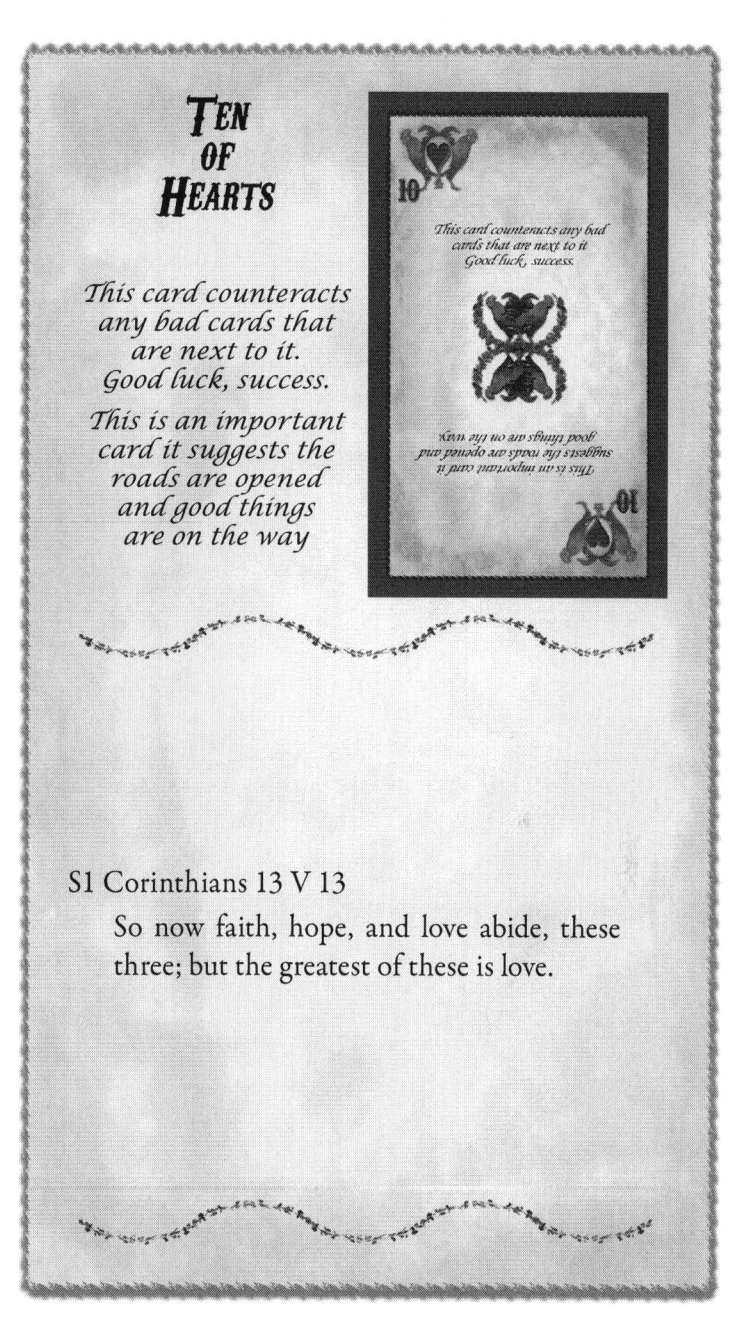

This card counteracts any bad cards that are next to it. Good luck, success.

This is an important card it suggests the roads are opened and good things are on the way

S1 Corinthians 13 V 13

So now faith, hope, and love abide, these three; but the greatest of these is love.

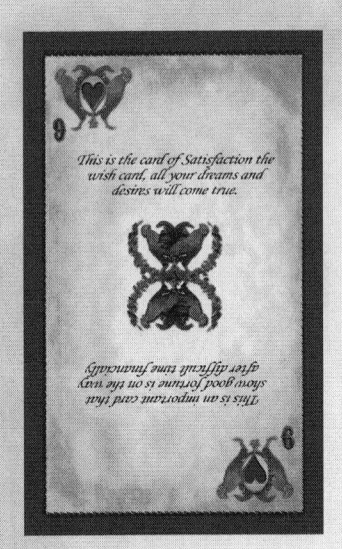

NINE OF HEARTS

This is the card of Satisfaction the wish card, all your dreams and desires will come true.

This is an important card that shows good fortune is on the way after difficult time financially

Isaiah 65 V 21-23

"And they shall build houses, and inhabit them; and they shall plant vineyards, and eat the fruit of them. They shall not build, and another inhabit; they shall not plant, and another eat: for as the days of a tree are the days of my people, and mine elect shall long enjoy the work of their hands. They shall not labour in vain, nor bring forth for trouble; for they are the seed of the blessed of the LORD, and their offspring with them."

Eight of Hearts

This is the card of movement. Things will final move in the direction you want them too

You have decided to leave the situation you are in and move forward

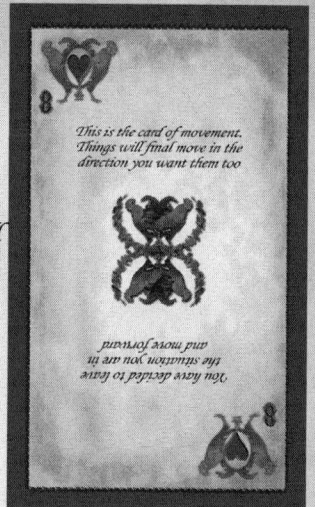

Hebrews 11 V 8-10

"By faith Abraham, when called to go to a place he would later receive as his inheritance, obeyed and went, even though he did not know where he was going. By faith he made his home in the promised land like a stranger in a foreign country; he lived in tents, as did Isaac and Jacob, who were heirs with him of the same promise. For he was looking forward to the city with foundations, whose architect and builder is God."

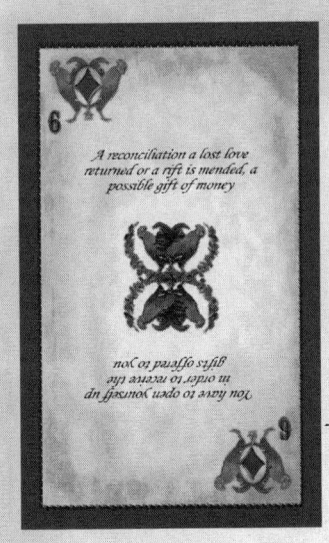

Seven of Hearts

This card represents total confusion. Take {7} spiritual baths for {7} days and read Isaiah 41 daily

An unreliable who is more an enemy than a friend, it's time to do a cut and clear remove yourself from the person or situation

On card (upright): *A reconciliation a lost love returned or a rift is mended, a possible gift of money*

On card (reversed): *You have to open yourself up in order to receive the gifts offered to you*

Proverbs 3 V 13-17

Happy is the man who finds skillful and godly Wisdom, and the man who gets understanding , For the gaining of it is better than the gaining of silver, and the profit of it better than fine gold. Skillful and godly Wisdom is more precious than rubies; and nothing you can wish for is to be compared to her. Length of days is in her right hand, and in her left hand are riches and honor.

Six of Hearts

It's time to let go of the past so you can move forward, Let go of the anger you are closing your own roads

Watch out for untrustworthy people, someone is trying to swindle you if you have spades around this card

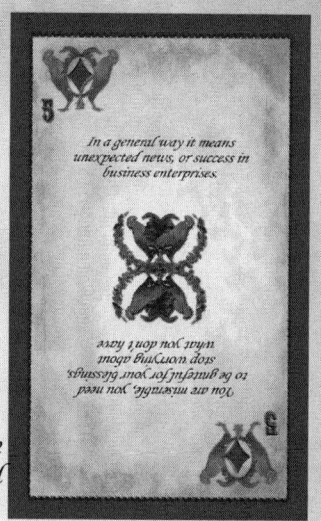

In a general way it means unexpected news, or success in business enterprises.

You are miserable, you need to be grateful for your blessings, stop worrying about what you don't have

2 Samuel 22 V 29

"For You are my lamp, O Lord; the Lord shall enlighten my darkness. For by You I can run against a troop; by my God I can leap over a wall. As for God, His way is perfect; the word of the Lord is proven; He is a shield to all who trust in Him."

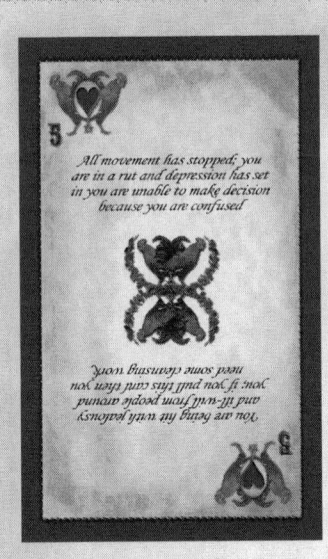

Five of Hearts

All movement has stopped; you are in a rut and depression has set in you are unable to make decision because you are confused

You are being hit with jealousy and ill-will from people around you; if you pull this card then you need some cleansing work

Lamentations 3 V 7-9

He has walled me in so I cannot escape; he has weighed me down with chains. Even when I call out or cry for help, he shuts out my prayer. He has barred my way with blocks of stone; he has made my paths crooked.

Four of Hearts

You have built walls around your heart and refuse to let changes come through for you, Change is coming so be opened to it

Postponements, delay's, there is a change in your home or business the cards surrounding you depend on the affect

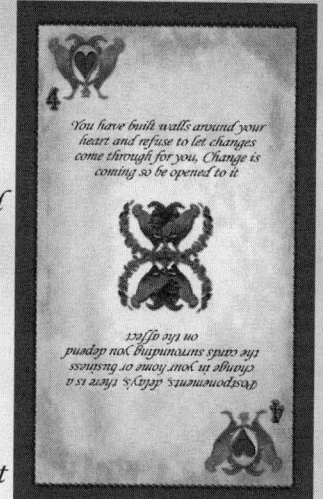

Isaiah 40 V 31

But those who wait for the Lord shall change and renew their strength and power; they shall lift their wings and mount up as eagles; they shall run and not be weary, they shall walk and not faint or become tired.

Three of Hearts

Be cautious don't make impulsive decisions, this card is warning you not to jump into anything. Think before you move

Confusion, you are unable to make a clear decision, this card also indicates emotional problems

Proverbs 2 V 10-11

For wisdom will enter your heart and knowledge will be pleasant to your soul. Discretion will protect you, and understanding will guard you.

Two of Hearts

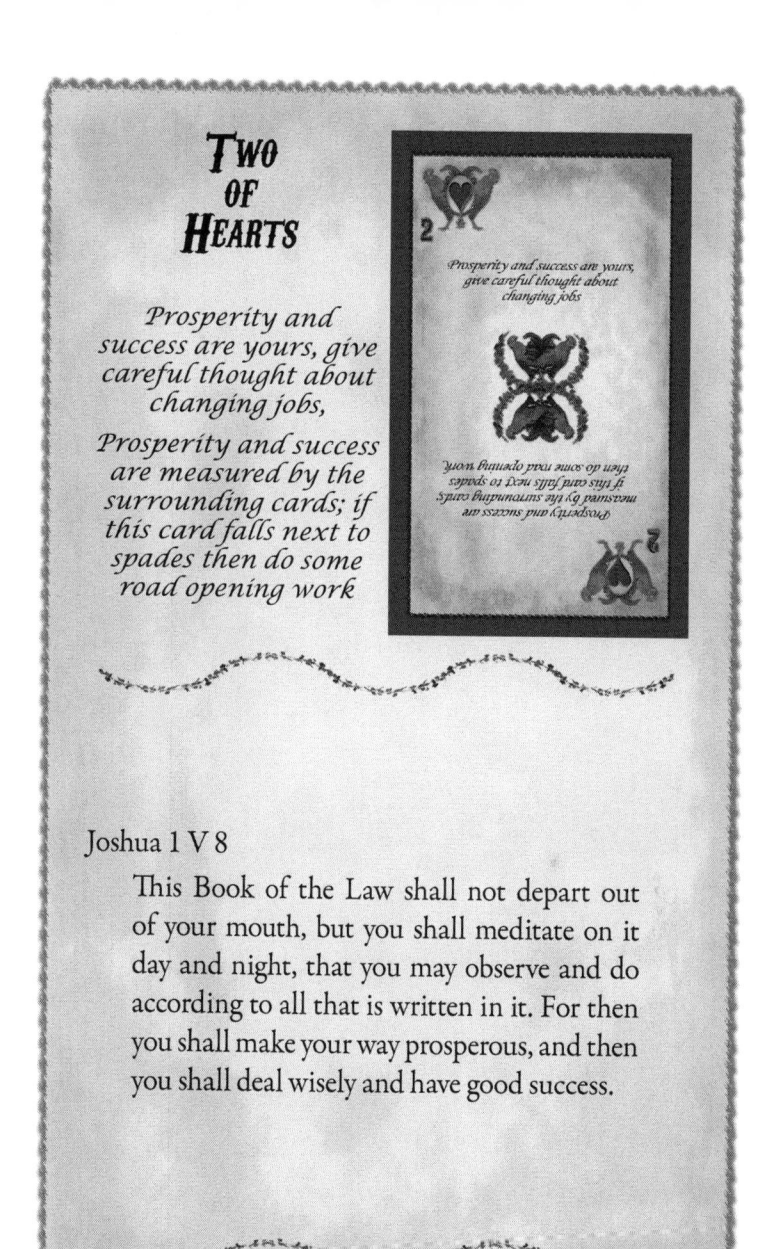

Prosperity and success are yours, give careful thought about changing jobs,

Prosperity and success are measured by the surrounding cards; if this card falls next to spades then do some road opening work

Joshua 1 V 8

This Book of the Law shall not depart out of your mouth, but you shall meditate on it day and night, that you may observe and do according to all that is written in it. For then you shall make your way prosperous, and then you shall deal wisely and have good success.

Ace of Clubs

Time to move into action, harmony, achievements, love, peace of mind, professional success

You are the only one who can hold yourself back, peaceful home, progress and success

Isaiah 32 V 17-18

The fruit of righteousness will be peace; the effect of righteousness will be quietness and confidence forever. My people will live in peaceful dwelling places, in secure homes, in undisturbed places of rest.

King of Clubs

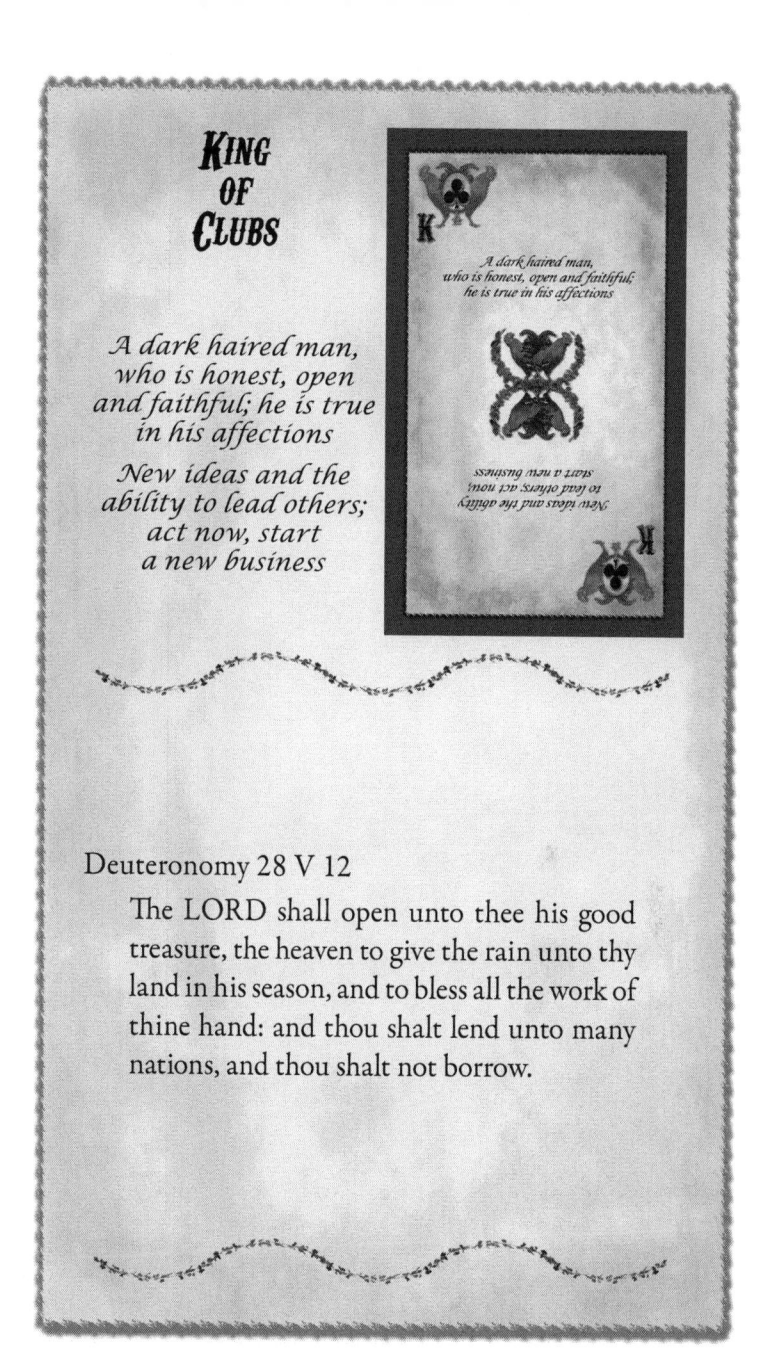

A dark haired man, who is honest, open and faithful; he is true in his affections

New ideas and the ability to lead others; act now, start a new business

Deuteronomy 28 V 12

> The LORD shall open unto thee his good treasure, the heaven to give the rain unto thy land in his season, and to bless all the work of thine hand: and thou shalt lend unto many nations, and thou shalt not borrow.

Queen of Clubs

A dark woman, strong willed, helpful, attractive, nice woman, but she is inclined to be moody

Time to move yourself up front and center; let the lime light shine on you

Isaiah 60 V 1-3

Arise, shine; for thy light is come, and the glory of the LORD is risen upon thee. For, behold, the darkness shall cover the earth, and gross darkness the people: but the LORD shall arise upon thee, and his glory shall be seen upon thee. And the Gentiles shall come to thy light, and kings to the brightness of thy rising.

Jack of Clubs

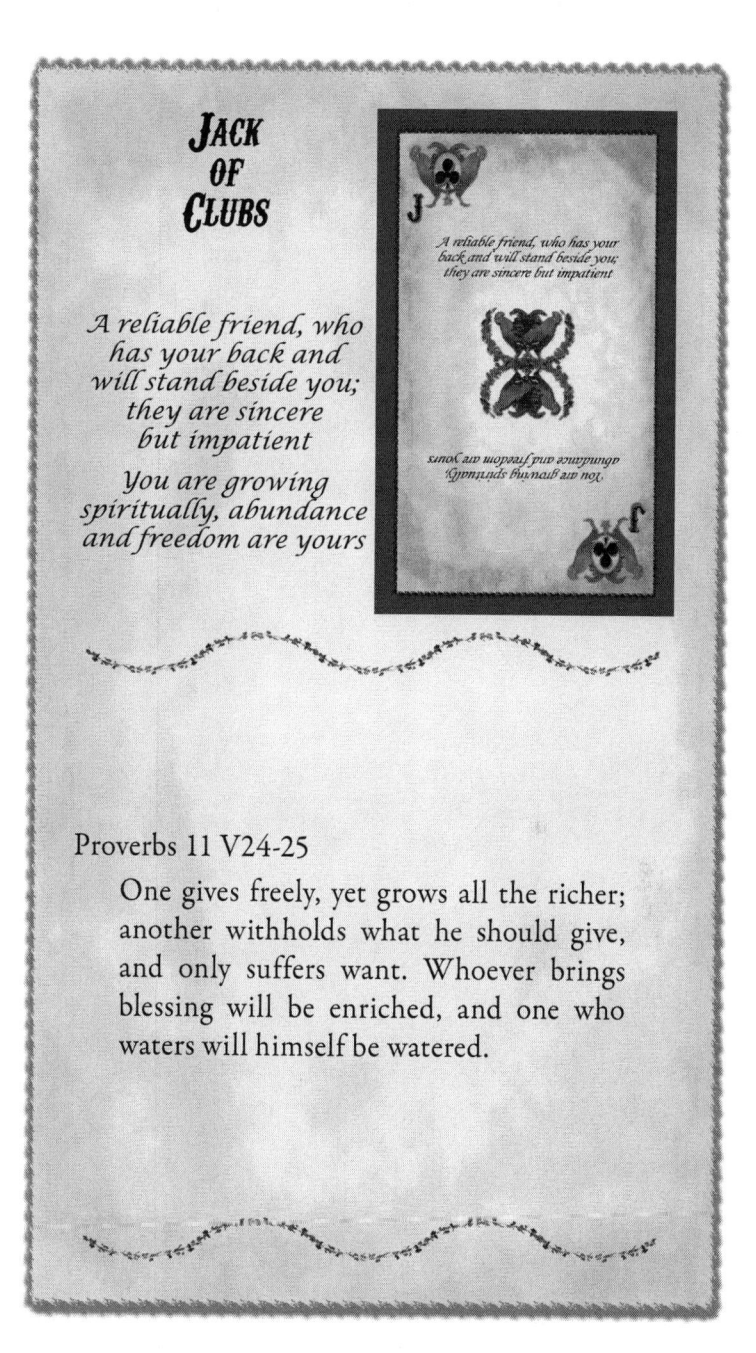

A reliable friend, who has your back and will stand beside you; they are sincere but impatient

You are growing spiritually, abundance and freedom are yours

Proverbs 11 V24-25

One gives freely, yet grows all the richer; another withholds what he should give, and only suffers want. Whoever brings blessing will be enriched, and one who waters will himself be watered.

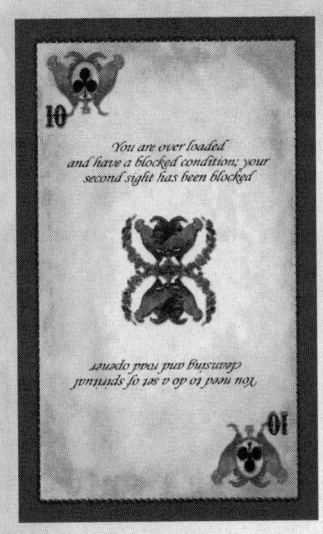

Ten of Clubs

You are over loaded and have a blocked condition; your second sight has been blocked

You need to do a set of spiritual cleansing and road opener

Hosea 6 V 1-3

Come, and let us return unto the LORD: for he hath torn, and he will heal us; he hath smitten, and he will bind us up. After two days will he revive us: in the third day he will raise us up, and we shall live in his sight. Then shall we know, if we follow on to know the LORD: his going forth is prepared as the morning; and he shall come unto us as the rain, as the latter and former rain unto the earth.

Nine of Clubs

You feel confused and are in a rut, disputes with friends over money

STOP, stand still and focus on your goal, do some spiritual cleansing

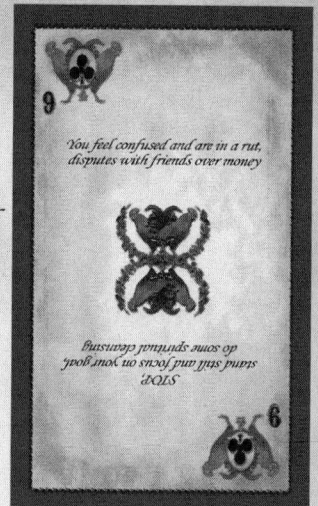

---

1 Kings 3 V 10-12

> The Lord was pleased that Solomon had asked for this. So God said to him, "Since you have asked for this and not for long life or wealth for yourself, nor have asked for the death of your enemies but for discernment in administering justice, I will do what you have asked. I will give you a wise and discerning heart, so that there will never have been anyone like you, nor will there ever be.

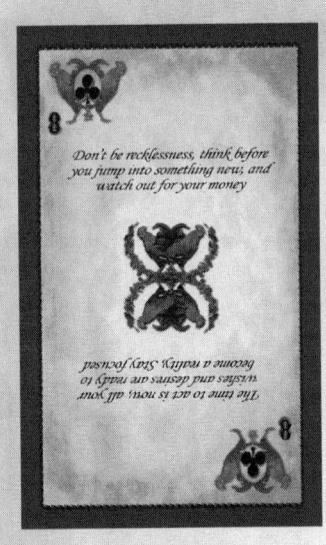

Eight of Clubs

Don't be recklessness, think before you jump into something new, and watch out for your money

The time to act is now, all your wishes and desires are ready to become a reality, Stay focused

Proverbs 27 V 23-24

Know well the condition of your flocks, and give attention to your herds, for riches do not last forever; and does a crown endure to all generations?

Seven of Clubs

You may have to defend yourself against an attack; you will be successful in removing ALL obstacles

It's time for defense and a strong wall of protection, you will be a success

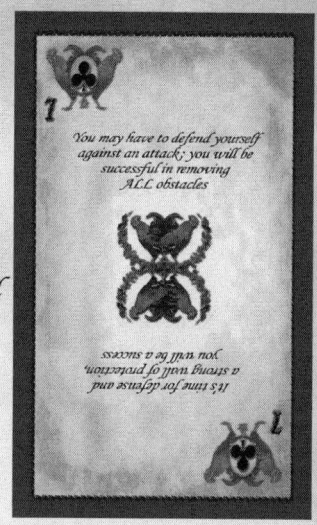

Exodus 15 V 6-7

> Thy right hand, O LORD, is become glorious in power: thy right hand, O LORD, hath dashed in pieces the enemy. And in the greatness of thine excellency thou hast overthrown them that rose up against thee: thou sentest forth thy wrath, which consumed them as stubble.

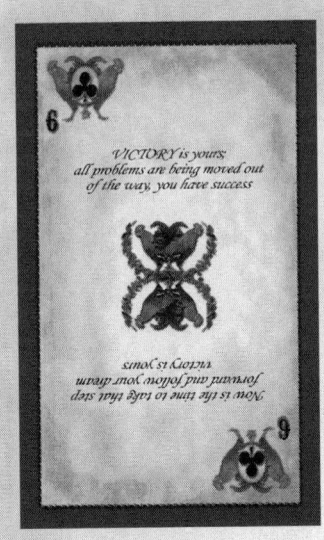

Six of Clubs

VICTORY is yours; all problems are being moved out of the way, you have success

Now is the time to take that step forward and follow your dream victory is yours

2 Chronicles 15 V 6-7

"One nation was being crushed by another and one city by another, because God was troubling them with every kind of distress. But as for you, be strong and do not give up, for your work will be rewarded."

Five of Clubs

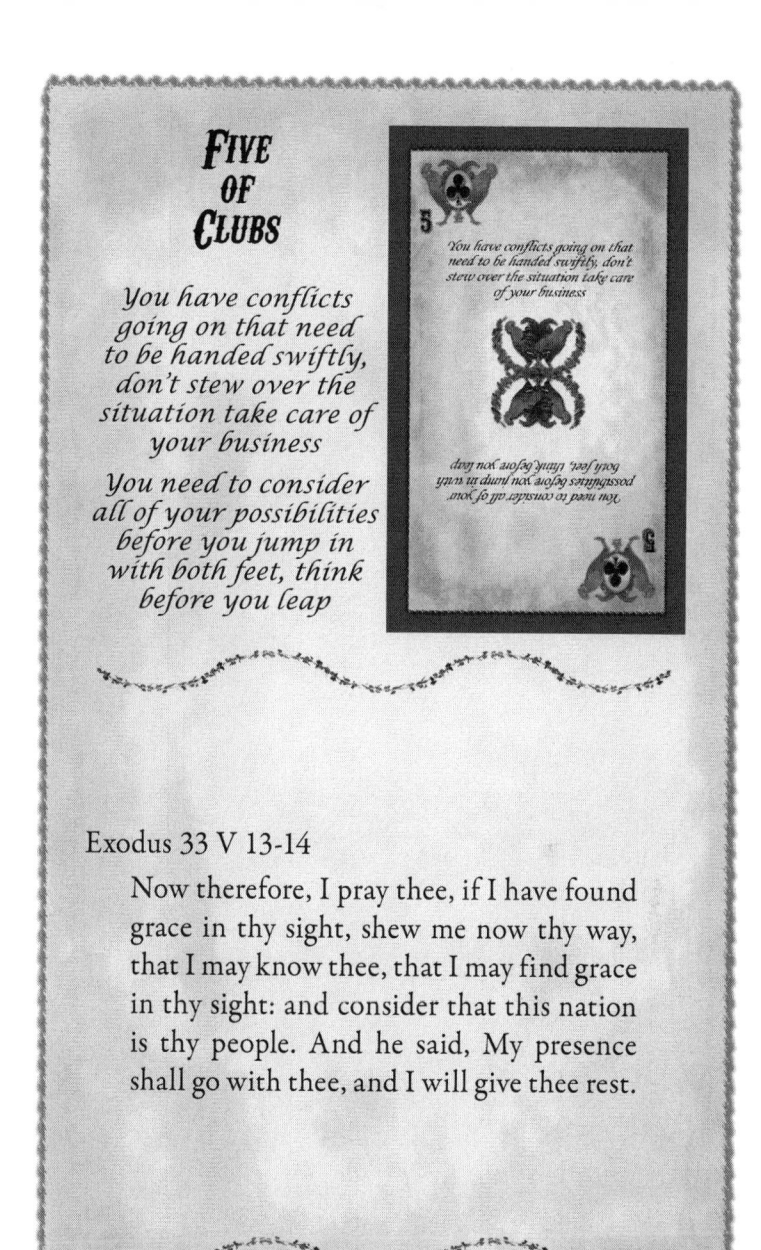

You have conflicts going on that need to be handed swiftly, don't stew over the situation take care of your business

You need to consider all of your possibilities before you jump in with both feet, think before you leap

Exodus 33 V 13-14

> Now therefore, I pray thee, if I have found grace in thy sight, shew me now thy way, that I may know thee, that I may find grace in thy sight: and consider that this nation is thy people. And he said, My presence shall go with thee, and I will give thee rest.

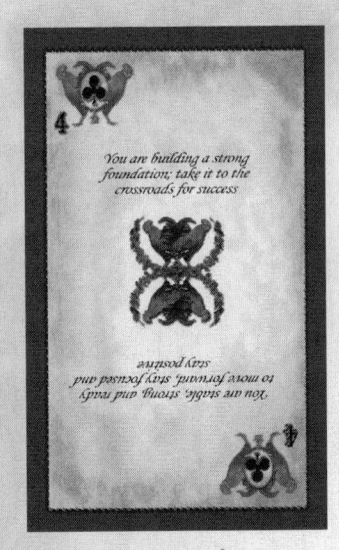

Four of Clubs

You are building a strong foundation; take it to the crossroads for success

You are stable, strong, and ready to move forward, stay focused and stay positive

Genesis 1 V 28

And God blessed them. And God said to them, "Be fruitful and multiply and fill the earth and subdue it and have dominion over the fish of the sea and over the birds of the heavens and over every living thing that moves on the earth."

Three of Clubs

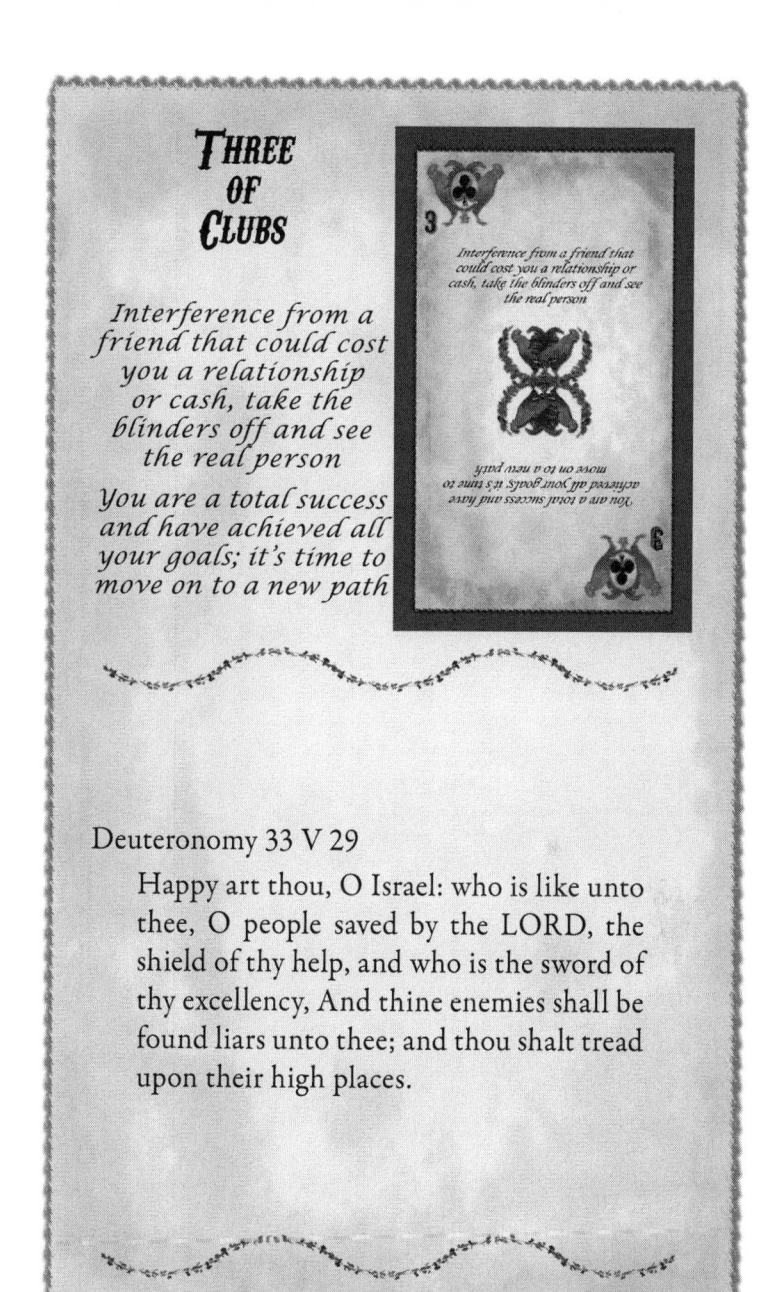

Interference from a friend that could cost you a relationship or cash, take the blinders off and see the real person

You are a total success and have achieved all your goals; it's time to move on to a new path

Deuteronomy 33 V 29

> Happy art thou, O Israel: who is like unto thee, O people saved by the LORD, the shield of thy help, and who is the sword of thy excellency, And thine enemies shall be found liars unto thee; and thou shalt tread upon their high places.

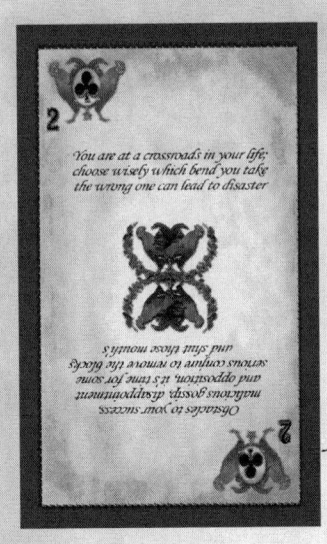

Two of Clubs

You are at a crossroads in your life; choose wisely which bend you take the wrong one can lead to disaster

Obstacles to your success, malicious gossip, disappointment and opposition, it's time for some serious conjure to remove the blocks and shut those mouth's

Numbers 10 V 9

And if ye go to war in your land against the enemy that oppresseth you, then ye shall blow an alarm with the trumpets; and ye shall be remembered before the LORD your God, and ye shall be saved from your enemies.

Ace of Spades

Crossed Conditions, Roads Closed, conflicts, a difficult love affair, this is a warning that troubles await the inquirer

Serious cleansing is needed here, followed by some protection conjure, follow through and you will make the right decisions

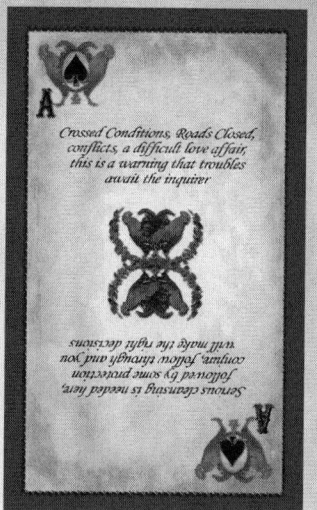

Ephesians 6 V 10

"Finally my brethren, be strong in the LORD and in the power of his might. Put on the whole armor of God that ye may be able to stand against the wiles of the devil. For we wrestle not against flesh and blood, but against powers, against the rulers of the darkness of this world, against spiritual wickedness in high places. Wherefore take unto you the whole armor of God that ye may be able to withstand in the evil day, and have done all, to stand."

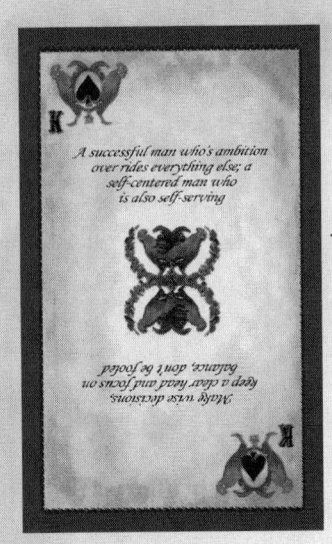

KING OF SPADES

A successful man who's ambition over rides everything else; a self-centered man who is also self-serving

Make wise decisions, keep a clear head and focus on balance, don't be fooled

Isaiah 2 V 11-12

"The lofty looks of man shall be humbled, and the haughtiness of men shall be bowed down, and the LORD alone shall be exalted in that day. For the day of the LORD of hosts shall be upon every one that is proud and lofty, and upon every one that is lifted up; and he shall be brought low."

Queen of Spades

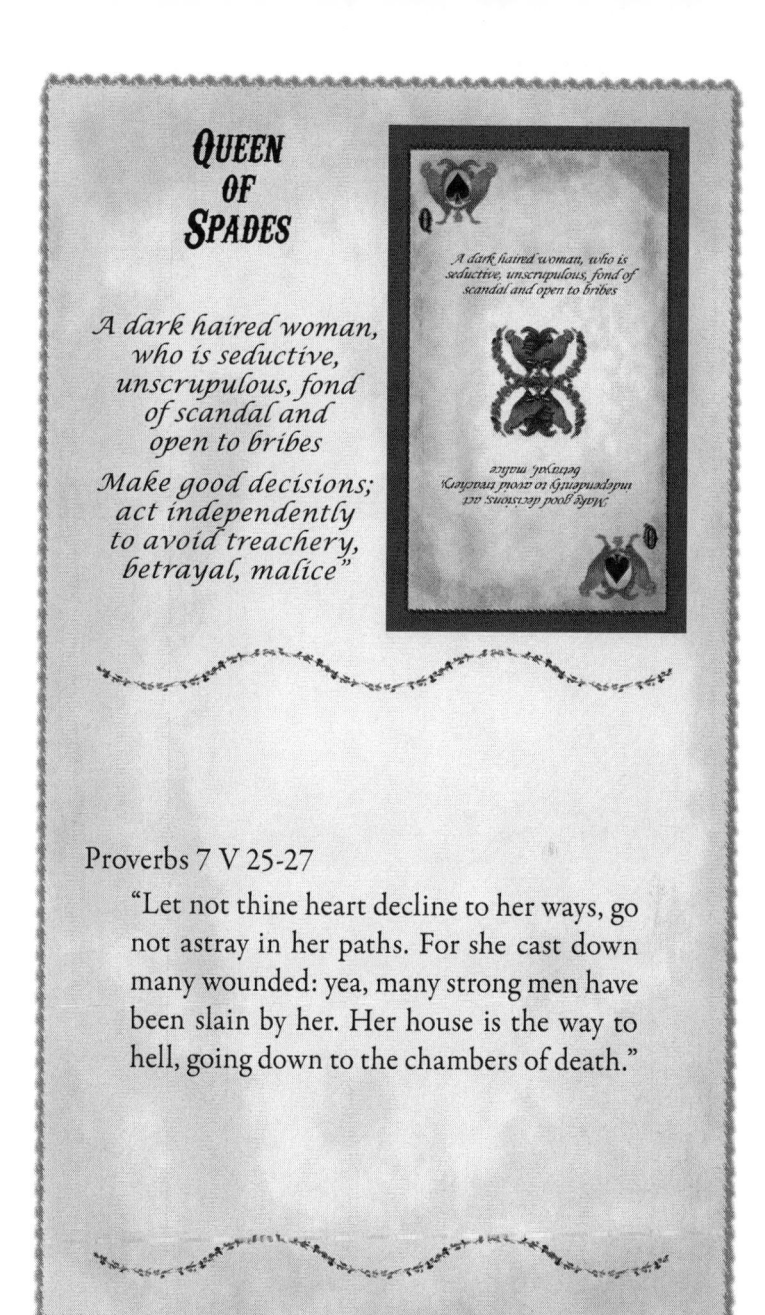

A dark haired woman, who is seductive, unscrupulous, fond of scandal and open to bribes

Make good decisions; act independently to avoid treachery, betrayal, malice

Proverbs 7 V 25-27

> "Let not thine heart decline to her ways, go not astray in her paths. For she cast down many wounded: yea, many strong men have been slain by her. Her house is the way to hell, going down to the chambers of death."

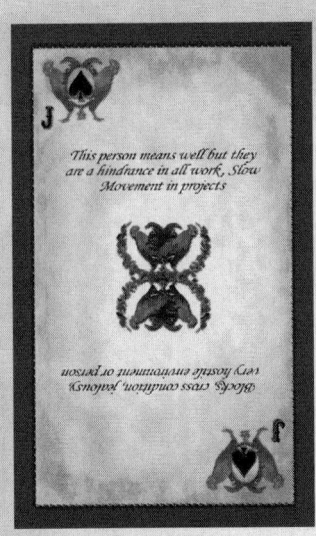

JACK OF SPADES

This person means well but they are a hindrance in all work. Slow movement in projects

Blocks, cross condition, jealousy, very hostile environment or person

---

Exodus 23 V 22

"If you listen carefully to what he says and do all that I say, I will be an enemy to your enemies and will oppose those who oppose you."

Ten of Spades

The quadrant is at his/her personal low with depression, worry, grief, and the imprisonment of their spirit

Bad News, Illness, An accident, Bad Luck, Jinxed, or crossed, you are moving too fast; slow down A strong Cleansing is needed

Proverbs 17 V 22

"A merry heart doeth good like a medicine: but a broken spirit drieth the bones."

{OR}

Jeremiah 29 V 11

"For I know the plans I have for you," declares the LORD, "plans to prosper you and not to harm you, plans to give you hope and a future."

Nine of Spades

Bad luck, delays, quarrels, sleeplessness sickness, losses, troubles, and family problems TAKE ACTION

If you draw this card then you need a strong spiritual cleansing you also need some strong protection work

Isaiah 40 V 31

"But those who hope in the LORD will renew their strength. They will soar on wings like eagles; they will run and not grow weary, they will walk and not be faint."

Eight of Spades

Two faced friends, disappointments and opposition, be cautious, A warning with regard to any business deals being worked on

This card close to the inquirer means a jinx, or crossed condition needs to be removed you have been nailed down

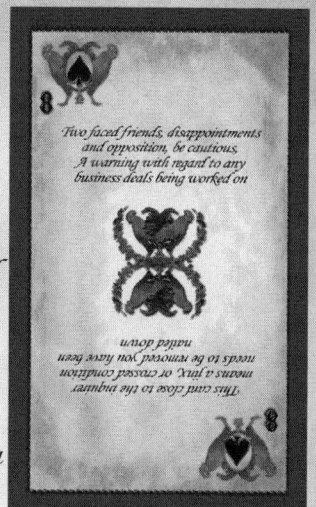

Isaiah 54 V 7

"No weapons formed against you shall prosper, and every tongue which rises against you in judgment you shall condemn. This is the heritage of the servants of the LORD, and their righteousness is from Me," says the LORD.

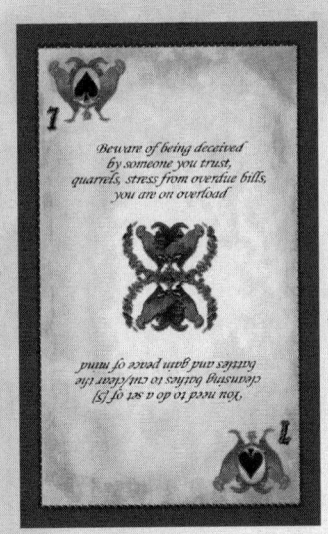

SEVEN OF SPADES

Beware of being deceived by someone you trust, quarrels, stress from overdue bills, you are on overload

You need to do a set of {5} cleansing bathes to cut/clear the battles and gain peace of mind

Deuteronomy 7 V 15

"And the LORD will take away from you all sickness, and will afflict you with none of the terrible diseases of Egypt which you have known, but will lay them on all those who hate you."

Six of Spades

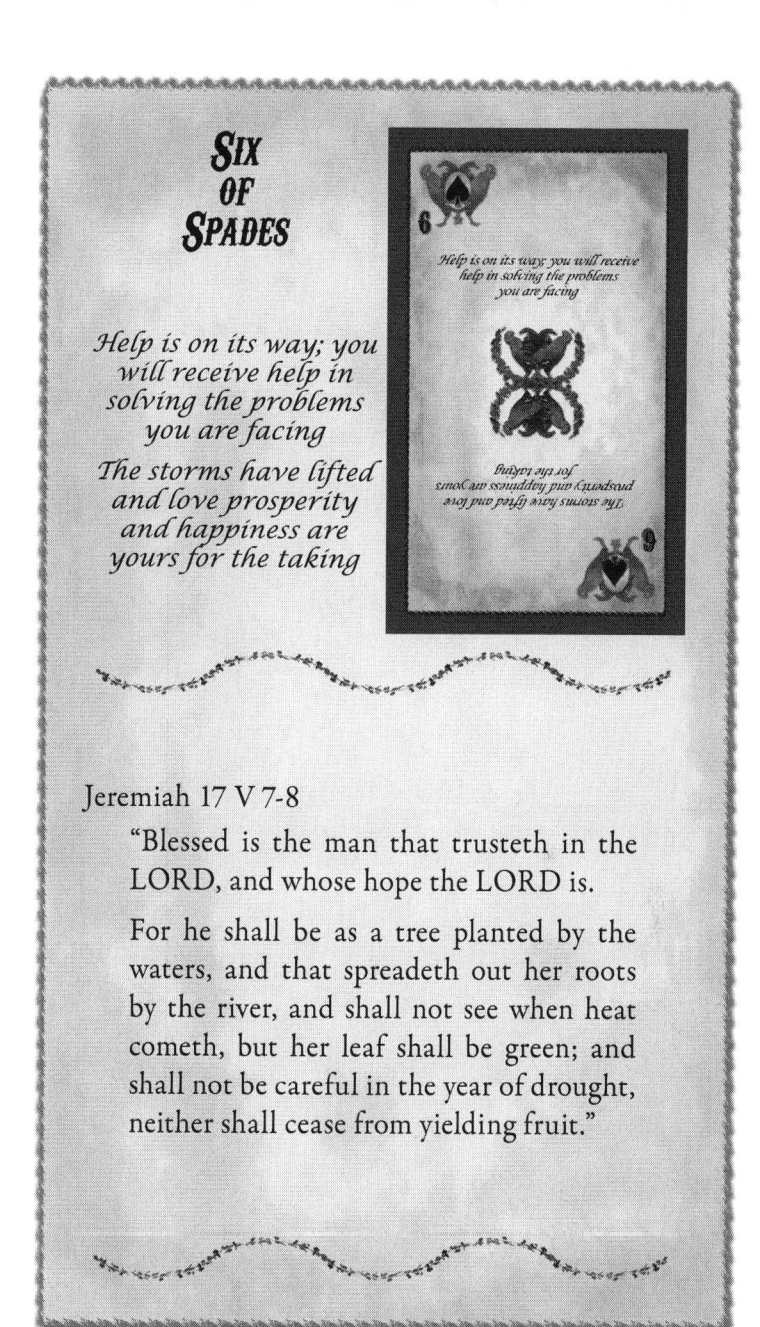

Help is on its way; you will receive help in solving the problems you are facing

The storms have lifted and love prosperity and happiness are yours for the taking

Jeremiah 17 V 7-8

"Blessed is the man that trusteth in the LORD, and whose hope the LORD is.

For he shall be as a tree planted by the waters, and that spreadeth out her roots by the river, and shall not see when heat cometh, but her leaf shall be green; and shall not be careful in the year of drought, neither shall cease from yielding fruit."

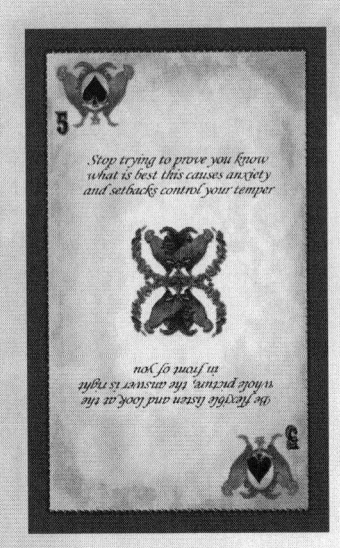

Five of Spades

Stop trying to prove you know what is best this causes anxiety and setbacks control your temper

Be flexible listen and look at the whole picture, the answer is right in front of you

Proverbs 3 V 5-6

Trust in the LORD with all thine heart; and lean not unto thine own understanding. In all thy ways acknowledge him, and he shall direct thy paths."

Four of Spades

Jealousy, business troubles, sickness, minor misfortunes or delays in a project

STOP! Be still and take the time to focus and relax you can fix the problem

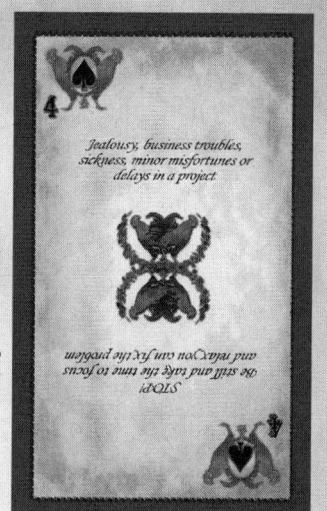

Isaiah 61 V 1-3

"The Spirit of the Lord God is upon me, because the Lord hath anointed me to bring good news to the poor; he has sent me to bind up the broken hearted, to proclaim liberty to the captives, and the opening of the prison to those who are bound; to proclaim the year of the Lord's favor, and the day of vengeance of our God; to comfort all who mourn; to grant to those who mourn in Zion—to give them a beautiful headdress instead of ashes, the oil of gladness instead of mourning, the garment of praise instead of a faint spirit; that they may be called oaks of righteousness, the planting of the Lord, that he may be glorified."

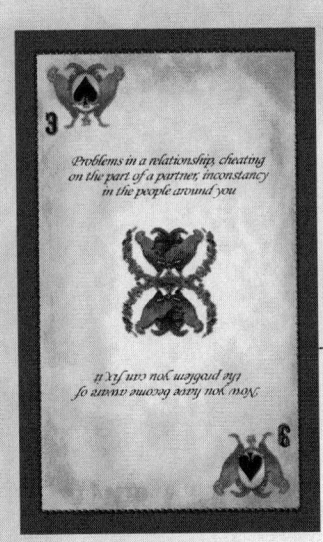

Three of Spades

Problems in a relationship, cheating on the part of a partner, inconstancy in the people around you

Now you have become aware of the problem you can fix it

Proverbs 10 V 9

"Whoever walks in integrity walks securely, but he who makes his ways crooked will be found out."

Two of Spades

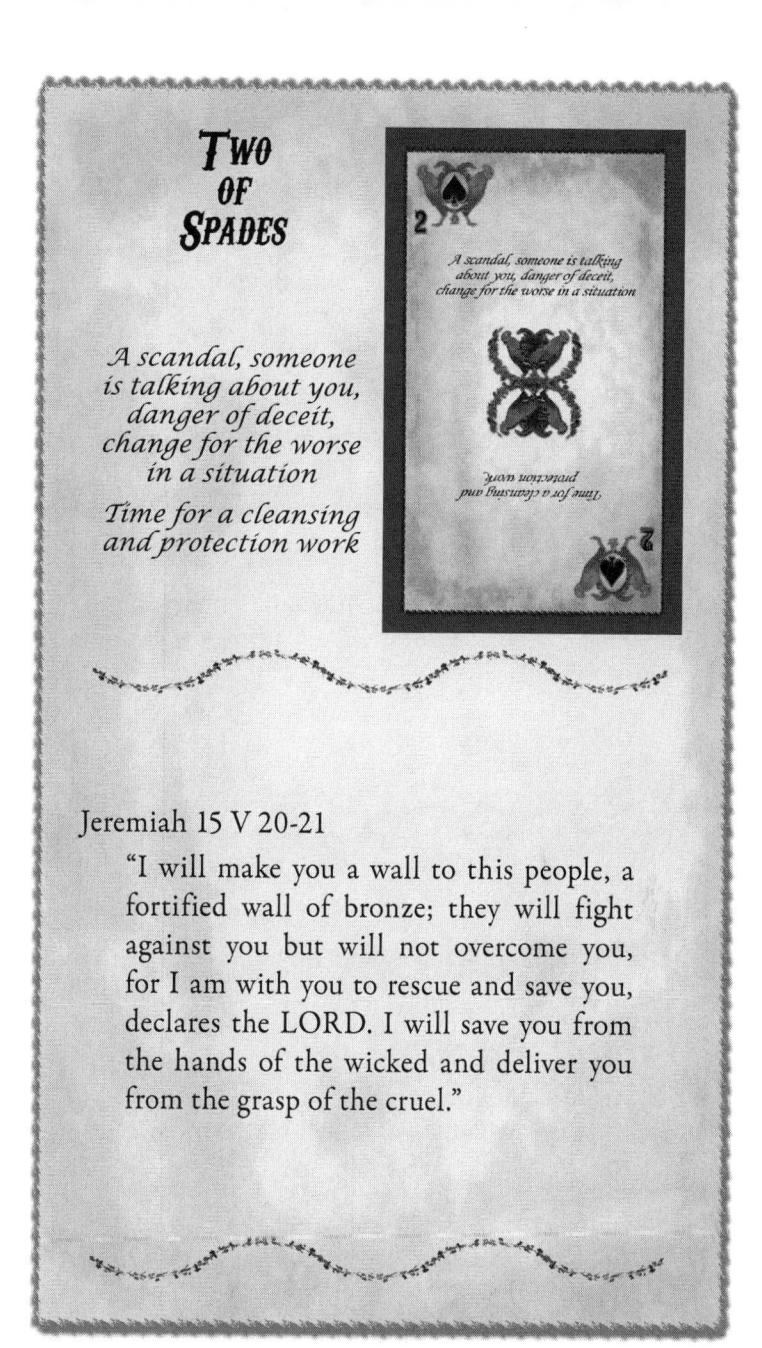

A scandal, someone is talking about you, danger of deceit, change for the worse in a situation

Time for a cleansing and protection work

Jeremiah 15 V 20-21

> "I will make you a wall to this people, a fortified wall of bronze; they will fight against you but will not overcome you, for I am with you to rescue and save you, declares the LORD. I will save you from the hands of the wicked and deliver you from the grasp of the cruel."

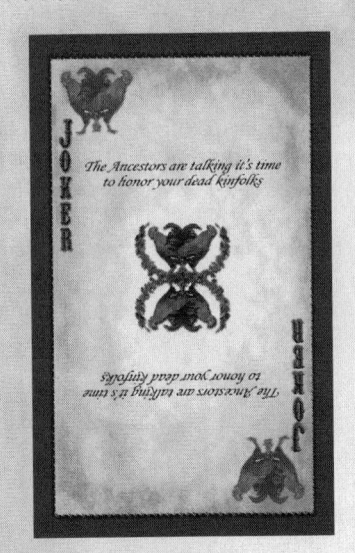

JOKER

The Ancestors are talking it's time to honor your dead kinfolks

Isaiah 26 V 19

But your dead will live, LORD; their bodies will rise let those who dwell in the dust wake up and shout for joy your dew is like the dew of the morning; the earth will give birth to her dead.

2 Corinthians 1 V 9-11

"But this happened that we might not rely on ourselves but on God, who raises the dead. He has delivered us from such a deadly peril, and he will deliver us. On him we have set our hope that he will continue to deliver us, as you help us by your prayers. Then many will give thanks on our behalf for the gracious favor granted us in answer to the prayers of many."

Card Combinations

There is more to reading the cards than understanding the meanings of the cards. You need to get a feel for the lay-outs and how the cards fall in a reading. Reading the cards is like putting a puzzle together. I have found that when certain cards fall together in a reading certain things seem to be going on. Below you will find a few combinations and how I see them. There are many more but these are just a small interpretation to give you an idea. They are not written in stone and you may read them differently.

Ace of Diamonds/Ten of Hearts —
>   If these two {2} cards fall together in a reading it could mean that the couple could be headed for marriage.

Ace of Diamonds/Ten of Diamonds —
: This marriage is for money only; if the seven {7} of Spades falls near then the person is being compelled into the marriage.

Ace of Diamonds/Six of Spades —
: Something is gonna cost you money; or you want get the raise you are looking for.

Ace of Diamonds/Seven of Hearts —
: You have a rival, if these cards fall next to the Ace of Hearts then it is someone after your lover.

Ace of Clubs among Diamonds —
: Total success

King, Queen or Jack between two cards of same number —
: Someone will offer you their support in a serious situation.

King or Queen between two Jacks —
: You need protection from your enemies

Queen of Spades between a King and a Queen —
: This gives us a warning of a possible relationship break-up.

Jack next to either King or Queen —
: You need protection work done.

Jack of Spades among several Diamonds —
: An argument about money.

Seven, Ten and Three of Diamonds —
: A secret will be told.

Seven and Eight of Diamonds —

Keep your business in your own house or it will be told. Gossip about you is running wild.

Eight and Nine of Spades —
(or Nine and Ten of Spades) This layout could be a warning of health problems.

Ten of Diamonds/Ten of Clubs —
You have the Midas touch.

Ten of Hearts/King & Queen of Hearts —
Possible wedding

Ten of Diamonds/Seven of Spades —
Road blocks and delays are in your way for success. Do a cleansing.

Five and Eight of Spades —
A jealous rival is stalking you, be very careful. It's time for a cut/clear.

Four of Diamonds and Four of Spades —
You are being crossed and forced to make a decision against your will.

Below are some more combinations of cards depending on how they fall in the reading. If they fall in Multiples of two {2}, three {3}, or four {4} in a reading the stronger the possibility is.

Ace	New Beginnings
	Reuniting
	Spades & Diamonds
	— difficult marriage or partnership
	Good News
	Lucky Break

2	Opposition
	Separation
	Reaching a crossroads
3	Roads are opened
	The line of Communications are opened
	Success
4	A Shaky foundation
	Crossed Condition
	Witchcraft
5	Change
	Roads are closed
	Disappointments
6	Contradictions
	Hard work
	Blocks
7	Gossip
	Brief Illnesses
	Someone is trying to set you up
8	Indiscretion
	Crossed Condition
	Blocks
9	Prosperity
	Good Health
	Roads are opened
10	Completion
	Circumstances improve
	Total Success

Jacks	Youth {Male or Female}
	Disagreements
	False friends
	Quarrels
	Battles
Queens	Mature Female
	{2} faced female friend
	Gossip
	Betrayal of Confidence
	Scandals
Kings	Mature Male
	Business partnership
	Support
	Success

Timing in Readings

Each set of suits of cards represent a certain time of year. The suit that shows up the most in a reading will give you an idea about when the event could happen.

> Diamonds — Spring
> Clubs — Autumn
> Hearts — Summer
> Spades — Winter

Months

Just like the suits that represent the time of year the suits can also represent the months of the year.

Below is a list to help you determine when the event may happen.

    Jack of Clubs —
            January, February, March

    Jack of Hearts —
            April, May, June

    Jack of Spades —
            July, August, September

    Jack of Diamonds —
            October, November, December

Closing

I hope you enjoy your deck of cards and the card kit. This has been in the making for about five {5} years; I just took my time. When you are reading cards remember that nothing is written in stone. You can change the outcome of any reading by changing your direction. With this deck of cards you can work the cards so the outcome is more to your liking, if you get a reading you are not happy with. The only person that can hold you back is you! Don't limit yourself. These are Conjure cards and will help you by tell you things that can help the situation.

"Blessings to all who read this book".
Momma Starr

OTHER RESOURCES

Along with Orion Foxwood (**OrionFoxwood.com**), Auntie Sindy Todo (**TodoMojo.com**) and Susan Diamond, I am a part of the annual *Conjure Con Festival* in Santa Cruz, where we provide hands-on workshops on various conjure techniques. You can find out more at **ConjureCon.com**.

The Serpent's Kiss, host of Conjure Con in Santa Cruz, Ca. is a valuable resource for quality hand crafted Conjure supplies. They even make their own Florida water and candles! For more information on events and products, visit **www.Serpents-Kiss.com**

The New Orleans FolkMagic Festival is an annual weekend intensive produced by Conjure Crossroads which consists of: Shimmering Wolf (*ShimmeringWolf.com*), Auntie Sindy Todo (*TodoMojo.com*), Susan Diamond (*Serpents-Kiss.com* and *2Hoodoos.com*), Orion Foxwood (*OrionFoxwood.com*) and Starr Casas (*OldStyleConjure.com*). This year 2013 is the 4th year.

Shimmering Wolf is the go to guy for all the events for Conjure Crossroads and Conjure Con. Wolf is the god of the web work, audio and video for these festivals. He can be contacted at *ShimmeringWolf.com*.

Priestess Miriam of the *Voodoo Spiritual Temple* in New Orleans LA is a deeply loved and respected Voodoo Mambo, and an educational resource on the syncretic nature and sacred practices of American Voodoo. Her temple and educational center is an invaluable resource. More information on Priestess Miriam and her temple can be found at *VoodooSpiritualTemple.org*.

When visiting New Orleans, one of the most resourceful and informed historians, tour guides, and New Orleans Voodoo Mambos you will find is Mary Milan, also known as *Bloody Mary of Bloody Mary's Tours*. For information on Mary and her tours, see *BloodyMarysTours.com*.

You can find out more about my dear friend **Orion Foxwood** and his Appalachian Southern Conjure at his website *OrionFoxwood.com*.

And of course, you can check out my products and services at my own website, *OldStyleConjure.com*.

About the Author

Starr Casas

I am an ol' Kentucky-born traditional Old Style Conjure woman who works with herbs, roots, and the Spirits. I am also known as a two headed root doctor and spiritual advisor. I learned how to do this work from my momma and grandmomma, who in turn, learned from their elders. Apart from my elders, I had wonderful folks coming into my life, who taught me hands on spiritual work.

Conjure, or what people now call Hoodoo, has always been around. In my family we didn't call it Hoodoo. We simply knew this to be "Conjure" or "work."

I have been a Conjure woman for over 50 years. I first learned how to read playing cards at 16, and by the time I was 17, I was already doing spiritual cleansings, or what some call uncrossing work, as well as healing work. At first I limited my work to the family, but when I turned 25, I knew it was time to start helping others. I began to do Conjure work full time for folks that were referred to me by my relatives or by others who knew me. I always worked only by word of mouth until three years ago, when I felt it was time to share my gift of Conjure work on the Internet.

I serve my community at my little shop where I offer consultations for those seeking help from a caring and compassionate spiritual worker. I also offer candle burning services to set a vigil light on troubles and concerns. I offer Conjure mini courses, as well as Old Style Conjure Oils, Conjure hands (mojo bags), Hoodoo prayer kits, Conjure bottles, and Conjure dollies to give power and domination. All of my products are blessed and prayed over by me to give clients the upper hand in all situations, to master their troubles and come out victorious, to be the leader that God wants them to be.

You can contact me at:

Website:
OldStyleConjure.com

Blog:
OldStyleConjure.blogspot.com

Blog:
Radio: BlogTalkRadio.com/OldStyleConjure

Etsy:
Etsy.com/shop/OldStyleConjure

Other Books by Starr Casas

OLD STYLE CONJURE WORKBOOK
Volume I
WORKING THE ROOT

Available through:

Pendraig Publishing

Magickal Works from Pendraig Publishing

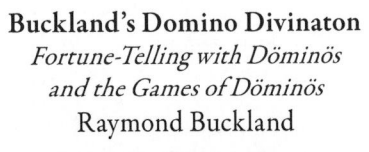

Balkan Traditional Witchcraft
Radomir Ristic

Buckland's Domino Divinaton
Fortune-Telling with Döminös and the Games of Döminös
Raymond Buckland

Buckland's Practical Color Magick
Raymond Buckland

Hedge-Rider
Witches and the Underworld
Eric De Vries

Magical Rites from the Crystal Well
The Classic Book for Witches and Pagans
Ed Fitch

Masks of the Muse
Building a relationship with the Goddess of the West
Veronica Cummer

Mastering the Mystical Heptarchy
Scott Stenwick

Scottish Herbs and Fairy Lore
Ellen Evert Hopman

Enchantment
The Witch's Art of Manipulation by Gesture, Gaze and Glamour
Peter Paddon

Sorgitzak: Old Forest Craft
*Stories and messages
from the gods of Old Europe*
Veronica Cummer

Dancing the Blood
Sorgitzak II
Veronica Cummer

Sybil Leek:
Out of the Shadows
Christine Jones

The Crooked Path
*Selected Transcripts from
the Crooked Path Podcast*
Peter Paddon

The Flaming Circle
*A Reconstruction of the
Old Ways of Britain and Ireland*
Robin Artisson

The Forge of Tubal Cain
*Southern California Witchcraft,
Roebuck, and the Clan of Tubal Cain*
Ann Finnin

The Horn of Evenwood
Robin Artisson

The Resurrection of the Meadow
Robin Artisson

To Fly By Night
An Anthology of Hedgewitchery
Veronica Cummer

Visceral Magick
*Bridging the Gap
Between Magic and Mundane*
Peter Paddon

Witching Way of the Hollow Hill
*The Gramarye of the Folk
Who Dwell Below the Mound*
Robin Artisson

Printed in Great Britain
by Amazon.co.uk, Ltd.,
Marston Gate.